T0322017

Wandering
Nowhere

Wandering Nowhere

A PERSONAL JOURNAL FOR EVERYDAY INSPIRATION

Alan Watts

RIDER

I

Rider, an imprint of Ebury Publishing
20 Vauxhall Bridge Road
London SW1V 2SA

Rider is part of the Penguin Random House group of companies
whose addresses can be found at global.penguinrandomhouse.com

Penguin
Random House
UK

First published in Great Britain in 2023 by Rider
First published in the United States of America in 2023
by Pantheon Books, an imprint of Random House,
a division of Penguin Random House LLC, New York.

www.penguin.co.uk

A CIP catalogue record for this book is available from the British Library

ISBN 9781846048258

Printed and bound in Great Britain by Clays Ltd, Elcograf S.p.A.

The authorised representative in the EEA is Penguin Random House
Ireland, Morrison Chambers, 32 Nassau Street, Dublin D02 YH68

Penguin Random House is committed to a sustainable future
for our business, our readers and our planet. This book is made
from Forest Stewardship Council® certified paper.

Alan Watts spent a lifetime bringing the practical wisdom and spiritual revelations of Zen Buddhism to Western readers. Watts wrote more than twenty-five books, and his work represents a treasury of enlightened personal thought, compassionate disruption of convention, and—quite simply—sage advice for a life well lived.

In the following pages, discover some of Watts's most salient and pithy philosophical observations. Whether you are familiar with his work or quite new to it, these inspiring messages will guide you in the mindful practice of journaling.

From the quotidian to the profound, these prompts for self-reflection touch on themes such as living for the present moment, liberating the mind from patterns of anxiety and self-consciousness, not being deceived by arbitrary separations prescribed by language and society, and leaving behind our assumptions to see things as they truly are: fleeting yet everlasting, simple but wondrous.

Haven't we
been here
before?

Wandering

Nowhere

Sorrow can only be compared with the *memory*
of joy, which is not at all the same thing
as joy itself.

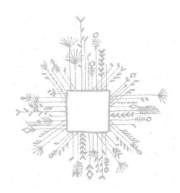

If the ego were to disappear or, rather, to be seen as a useful fiction, there would no longer be the duality of subject and object, experiencer and experience. There would simply be a continuous, self-moving stream of experiencing, without the sense either of an active subject who controls it or of a passive subject who suffers it. The thinker would be seen to be no more than the series of thoughts, and the feeler no more than the feelings.

One who talked incessantly, without stopping
to look and listen, would repeat himself
ad nauseam. It is the same with thinking,
which is really silent talking. It is not, by itself,
open to the discovery of anything new, for its
only novelties are simply rearrangements of
old words and ideas.

There is only this *now*.

To be forever looking beyond is to remain blind
to what is here.

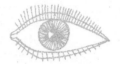

So long as one thinks about listening, one cannot hear clearly, and so long as one thinks about trying or not trying to let go of oneself, one cannot let go. Yet whether one thinks about listening or not, the ears are hearing just the same, and nothing can stop the sound from reaching them.

The more we try to live in the world of words,
the more we feel isolated and alone, the more all
the joy and liveliness of things is exchanged for
mere certainty and security.

Real religion is the transformation
of anxiety into laughter.

No one is more dangerously insane than one who is sane all the time: he is like a steel bridge without flexibility, and the order of his life is rigid and brittle.

The inevitability of pain will not be met by deadening sensitivity but by increasing it, by exploring and feeling out the manner in which the natural organism itself wants to react and which its innate wisdom has provided.

When thought stops from exhaustion, the mind is open to see the problem as it is—not as it is verbalized—and at once it is understood.

As far as we can judge, every animal is so busy with what he is doing at the moment that it never enters his head to ask whether life has a meaning or a future. For the animal, happiness consists in enjoying life in the immediate present—not in the assurance that there is a whole future of joys ahead of him.

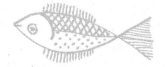

The realm of liberation is absolutely incommensurable with the relativities of higher and lower, better and worse, gain and loss, since these are all the transparent and empty advantages and disadvantages of the ego.

Not content with tasting the food, I am also trying to taste my tongue. Not content with feeling happy, I want to feel myself feeling happy—so as to be sure not to miss anything.

The rift between God and nature would vanish if we knew how to experience nature, because what keeps them apart is not a difference of substance but a split in the mind.

I have no other self than the totality of things
of which I am aware.

There are, then, two ways of understanding an experience. The first is to compare it with the memories of other experiences, and so to name and define it. This is to interpret it in accordance with the dead and the past. The second is to be aware of it as it is, as when, in the intensity of joy, we forget past and future, let the present be all, and thus do not even stop to think, "I am happy."

Life requires no future to complete itself
nor explanation to justify itself. In this moment
it is finished.

It does not seem to occur to us that action goaded by a sense of inadequacy will be creative only in a limited sense. It will express the emptiness from which it springs rather than fullness, hunger rather than strength.

Running away from fear is fear, fighting pain is pain, trying to be brave is being scared. If the mind is in pain, the mind is pain.

The point of music is discovered in every moment of playing and listening to it.

Feelings both positive and negative come and go without turmoil, for they seem to be simply observed, though there is no one observing. They pass trackless like birds in the sky, and build up no resistances which have to be dissipated in reckless action.

We want the protection of being "exclusive" and "special," seeking to belong to the safest church, the best nation, the highest class, the right set, and the "nice" people. These defenses lead to divisions between us, and so to more insecurity demanding more defenses. Of course it is all done in the sincere belief that we are trying to do the right things and live in the best way; but this, too, is a contradiction.

I cannot throw a ball so long as I am holding on to it—so as to maintain perfect control of its movement.

We keep reactivating the past in the hope that history is guiding us to where we should be going in the future, and this is driving the car with eyes glued to the rear-vision mirror.

A world which increasingly consists of
destinations without journeys between them,
a world which values only "getting somewhere"
as fast as possible, becomes a world
without substance.

The spiritual is not to be separated from the material, nor the wonderful from the ordinary.

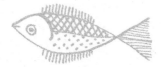

The anxiety-laden problem of what will happen
to me when I die is, after all, like asking what
happens to my fist when I open my hand,
or where my lap goes when I stand up.

To understand music, you must listen to it.
But so long as you are thinking, "I am listening
to this music," you are not listening.

I have had the privilege, especially in recent years, of seeing what I believe to be very deeply into the heart of this universe and its life—and there isn't anything to be afraid of. The end and bottom of it all is not emptiness, but a love beyond anyone's imagination.

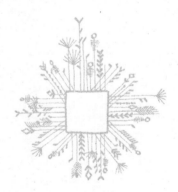

The harsh divisions of spirit and nature, mind and body, subject and object, controller and controlled, are seen more and more to be awkward conventions of language.

Nirvana can only arise unintentionally, spontaneously, when the impossibility of self-grasping has been thoroughly perceived.

Not to cherish both the angel and the animal,
both the spirit and the flesh, is to renounce the
whole interest and greatness of being human,
and it is really tragic that those in whom
the two natures are equally strong should be
made to feel in conflict with themselves.

Death is the unknown in which all of us
lived before birth.

It is only through silence that one can discover something new to talk about.

A living body is not a fixed *thing* but a flowing *event*, like a flame or a whirlpool.

If happiness always depends on something expected in the future, we are chasing a will-o'-the-wisp that ever eludes our grasp, until the future, and ourselves, vanish into the abyss of death.

Much of the secret of life consists in knowing how to laugh, and also how to breathe.

In a culture where sex is calculated, religion decorous, dancing polite, music refined or sentimental, and yielding to pain shameful, many people have never experienced full spontaneity.

What we have forgotten is that thoughts and
words are *conventions*, and that it is fatal to
take conventions too seriously. A convention is
a social convenience, as, for example, money . . .
But it is absurd to take money too seriously,
to confuse it with real wealth.

The frightened mind that runs away from everyday terrors meets the seeking mind that wants a better world.

The true splendor of science is not so much that it names and classifies, records and predicts, but that it observes and desires to know the facts, whatever they may turn out to be.

If a problem can be solved at all, to understand it
and to know what to do about it are the
same thing.

A mind that is single and sincere is not interested in being good, in conducting relations with other people so as to live up to a rule. Nor, on the other hand, is it interested in being free, in acting perversely just to prove its independence. Its interest is not in itself, but in the people and problems of which it is aware; these are "itself."

To see the light, it is only necessary to stop
dreaming and open the eyes.

We must see that consciousness is neither an isolated soul nor the mere function of a single nervous system, but of that totality of interrelated stars and galaxies which makes a nervous system possible.

The words which one might be tempted
to use for a silent and wide-open mind are
mostly terms of abuse—thoughtless, mindless,
unthinking, empty-headed, and vague. Perhaps
this is some measure of an innate fear of
releasing the chronic cramp of consciousness
by which we grasp the facts of life and
manage the world.

Hurrying and delaying are alike ways of trying
to resist the present.

Egoism is like trying to swim without relying on the water, endeavoring to keep afloat by tugging at your own legs; your whole body becomes tense, and you sink like a stone.

A way of liberation can have no positive definition. It has to be suggested by saying what it is not, somewhat as a sculptor reveals an image by the act of removing pieces of stone from a block.

The ego is the social image or role with which
the mind is shamed into identifying itself,
since we are taught to act the part which
society wants us to play—the part of a reliable
and predictable center of action which resists
spontaneous change.

A man rings like a cracked bell when he thinks
and acts with a split mind.

A certain amount of "sitting just to sit" might well be the best thing in the world for the jittery minds and agitated bodies.

When we have made up our minds as to what we *do* want, there remain indeed many practical and technical problems. But there is no point at all in discussing these until we have made up our minds.

If you try to capture running water in a bucket, it is clear that you do not understand it and that you will always be disappointed, for in the bucket the water does not run.

If, then, my awareness of the past and future makes me less aware of the present, I must begin to wonder whether I am actually living in the real world.

The ego-self constantly pushes reality away.
It constructs a future out of empty expectations
and a past out of regretful memories.

Nothing worthwhile is ever achieved
without danger.

What is true and positive is too real and too living to be described, and to try to describe it is like putting red paint on a red rose.

Faith is not clinging but letting go.

When a man no longer confuses himself with the definition of himself that others have given him, he is at once universal and unique.

A human being must always recognize that he is qualitatively more than any system of thought he can imagine, and therefore he should never label himself. He degrades himself when he does.

The brain can only assume its proper behavior when consciousness is doing what it is designed for: not writhing and whirling to get out of present experience, but being effortlessly aware of it.

As water seeks the course of least resistance, so the emotions clothe themselves in the symbols that lie most readily to hand, and the association is so swift and automatic that the symbol may appear to be the very heart of the experience.

There is no other reality than present reality,
so that, even if one were to live for endless ages,
to live for the future would be to miss the point
everlastingly.

The clash between science and religion has not shown that religion is false and science is true. It has shown that all systems of definition are relative to various purposes, and that none of them actually "grasp" reality.

Intelligence, which is in some sense systemic doubt, cannot proceed without also having to embrace its polar opposite—instinctual faith.

Muddy water is best cleared by leaving it alone.

Hell is the fatuity, the everlasting impossibility,
of self-love, self-consciousness, and
self-possession. It is trying to see one's own eyes,
hear one's own ears, and kiss one's own lips.

To be afraid of life is to be afraid of yourself.

The perishability and changefulness of the world are part and parcel of its liveliness and loveliness.

One of the greatest pains is to be self-conscious, to feel unabsorbed and cut off from the community and the surrounding world.

To travel is to be alive, but to get somewhere
is to be dead, for as our own proverb says,
"To travel well is better than to arrive."

It is in vain that we can predict and control the course of events in the future, unless we know how to live in the present. It is in vain that doctors prolong life if we spend the extra time being anxious to live still longer. It is in vain that engineers devise faster and easier means of travel if the new sights that we see are merely sorted and understood in terms of old prejudices.

Music is a delight because of its rhythm
and flow. Yet the moment you arrest the flow
and prolong a note or chord beyond its time,
the rhythm is destroyed.

You didn't come into this world. You came out of it, like a wave from the ocean. You are not a stranger here.

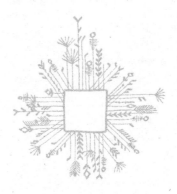

There is a point where thinking—like boiling an egg—must come to a stop.

The thinker has no other form than his thought.

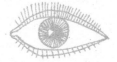

The answer to the problem of suffering is not
away from the problem but in it.

There is simply experience. There is not something or someone experiencing experience! You do not feel feelings, think thoughts, or sense sensations any more than you hear hearing, see sight, or smell smelling. "I feel fine" means that a fine feeling is present. It does not mean that there is one thing called an "I" and another separate thing called a feeling, so that when you bring them together this "I" *feels* the fine feeling.

When life is empty, with respect to the past, and aimless, with respect to the future, the vacuum is filled by the present—normally reduced to a hairline, a split second in which there is no time for anything to happen.

We get such a kick out of looking forward to
pleasures and rushing ahead to meet them that
we can't slow down enough to enjoy them when
they come.

According to convention, I am not simply what I am doing now. I am also what I have done, and my conventionally edited version of my past is made to seem almost more the real "me" than what I am at this moment. For what I *am* seems so fleeting and intangible, but what I *was* is fixed and final. It is the firm basis for predictions of what I will be in the future, and so it comes about that I am more closely identified with what no longer exists than with what actually is!

Our problem is that our long indoctrination in dualistic thinking has made it a matter of common sense that we can control our nature only by going against it. But this is the same false common sense which urges the driver to turn against the skid.

To get rid of what is passed on to you, you have
to develop a forgettory instead of a memory.

When you try to stay on the surface of the water, you sink; but when you try to sink, you float. When you hold your breath, you lose it—which immediately calls to mind an ancient and much neglected saying, "Whosoever would save his soul shall lose it."

The adept in Zen is one who manages to be human with the same artless grace and absence of inner conflict with which a tree is a tree. Such a man is likened to a ball in a mountain stream, which is to say that he cannot be blocked, stopped, or embarrassed in any situation.

Sexuality is not a separate compartment of human life; it is a radiance pervading every human relationship, but assuming a particular intensity at certain points.

If the universe is meaningless, so is the statement that it is so. If this world is a vicious trap, so is its accuser, and the pot is calling the kettle black.

There is never anything but the present,
and if one cannot live there, one cannot
live anywhere.

The greater the scientist, the more he is impressed with his ignorance of reality, and the more he realizes that his laws and labels, descriptions and definitions, are the products of his own thought.

Zen is a liberation from time. For if we open our eyes and see clearly, it becomes obvious that there is no other time than this instant, and that the past and the future are abstractions without any concrete reality.

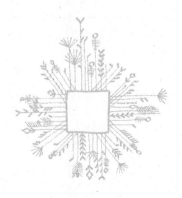

It is high time to ask whether it is really any scandal, any deplorable inconsistency, for a human being to be both angel and animal with equal devotion.

We have never ... permitted ourselves to be everything that we are, to see that fundamentally all the gains and losses, rights and wrongs, of our lives are as natural and "perfect" as the peaks and valleys of a mountain range.

The more a person knows of himself, the more he will hesitate to define his nature and to assert what he must necessarily feel, and the more he will be astounded at his capacity to feel in unsuspected and unpredictable ways.

You do not play a sonata *in order* to reach the final chord, and if the meanings of things were simply in ends, composers would write nothing but finales.

To be free from convention is not to spurn it but
not to be deceived by it. It is to be able to use it
as an instrument instead of being used by it.

To act or grow creatively we must begin from where we are, but we cannot begin at all if we are not "all here" without reservation or regret.

The only way to make sense out of change is to plunge into it, move with it, and join the dance.

In attachment there is pain, and in pain
deliverance, so that at this point attachment
itself offers no obstacle, and the liberated one
is at last free to love with all his might and to
suffer with all his heart.

We do not dance to reach a certain point on the floor, but simply to dance.

If we are open only to discoveries which will accord with what we know already, we may as well stay shut.

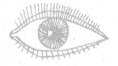

This—the immediate, everyday, and present experience—is IT, the entire and ultimate point for the existence of a universe.

The complexity of nature is not innate but a consequence of the instruments used to handle it. There is nothing complex about walking, breathing, and circulating one's blood. Living organisms have developed these functions without thinking about them at all.

Once the mind has seen through all fear and all
hope, it finds peace within itself, in a state
of awareness beyond thought.

A life full of goals or end-points is like trying
to abate one's hunger by eating merely the two
precise ends of a banana.

Only doubtful truths need defense.

Paradox as it may seem, we likewise find life meaningful only when we have seen that it is without purpose, and know the "mystery of the universe" only when we are convinced that we know nothing about it at all.

The more we struggle for life (as pleasure), the more we are actually killing what we love.

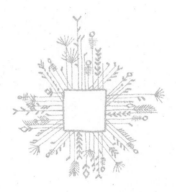

How long have the planets been circling the sun?
Are they getting anywhere, and do they go faster
and faster in order to arrive? How often has the
spring returned to the earth? Does it come faster
and fancier every year, to be sure to be better
than last spring, and to hurry on its way to the
spring that shall out-spring all springs?

One has only to consider how cold and desolate the fairest face of nature can seem to a man left utterly alone, willing to exchange the whole sum of natural beauty for a single human face.

Normally we do not so much look at things
as overlook them.

A clock is a convenient device for arranging to meet a friend, or for helping people to do things together, although things of this kind happened long before they were invented. Clocks should not be smashed; they should simply be kept in their place. And they are very much out of place when we try to adapt our biological rhythms of eating, sleeping, evacuation, working, and relaxing to their uniform circular rotation. Our slavery to these mechanical drill masters has gone so far and our whole culture is so involved with it that reform is a forlorn hope; without them civilization would collapse entirely. A less brainy culture would learn to synchronize its body rhythms rather than its clocks.

The paradox about waking up—I mean the ordinary kind of waking up that occurred to you and me this morning—is that you can't make it happen, yet it's inevitable. The same holds true spiritually. You can't wish, pray, beg, force, or meditate yourself awake.

The joy of travel is not nearly so much in getting where one wants to go as in the unsought surprises which occur on the journey.

The desire for security and the feeling of insecurity are the same thing. To hold your breath is to lose your breath.

Haven't we
been here
before?

NOTES

The philosopher Alan Watts (1915–1973) is best known for popularizing Zen Buddhism in the United States and Europe. During his lifetime he wrote more than twenty-five books, including the bestsellers *The Way of Zen* and *The Wisdom of Insecurity*. Born in England, Watts immigrated to the United States in his twenties. His colorful and controversial life, from his school days in England, to his priesthood in the Anglican Church as chaplain of Northwestern University, to his experimentation with psychedelic drugs, made him an icon of the 1960s counterculture movement. Millions of followers continue to be enlightened by his teachings through his books, which have been published in twenty-six countries, and his lectures, which are found worldwide on the internet.